SNAPSHOTS IN HISTORY

THE TEAPOT DOME SCANDAL

Corruption Rocks 1920s America

KENT MIDDLE SCHOOL
250 Stadium Way
Kentfield, CA 94904

by Barbara J. Davis

THE TEAPOT DOME SCANDAL

Corruption Rocks 1920s America

by Barbara J. Davis

Content Adviser: Derek Shouba, History Professor
and Assistant Provost, Roosevelt University

Reading Adviser: Alexa L. Sandmann, Ph.D.,
Associate Professor of Literacy, Kent State University

Compass Point Books ✦ Minneapolis, Minnesota

✦ COMPASS POINT BOOKS

3109 West 50th Street, #115
Minneapolis, MN 55410

This book was manufactured with paper containing
at least 10 percent post-consumer waste.

For Compass Point Books
Jennifer VanVoorst, Jaime Martens, Lori Bye, XNR Productions, Inc.,
Catherine Neitge, Keith Griffin, and Nick Healy

Produced by White-Thomson Publishing Ltd.
For White-Thomson Publishing
Stephen White-Thomson, Susan Crean, Amy Sparks,
Tinstar Design Ltd., Derek Shouba, Peggy Bresnick Kendler,
Brian Fitzgerald, Barbara Bakowski, and Timothy Griffin

Library of Congress Cataloging-in-Publication Data
Davis, Barbara.
The Teapot Dome Scandal : corruption rocks 1920s America / by
Barbara Davis.
     p. cm. — (Snapshots in history)
  ISBN-13: 978-0-7565-3336-6 (library binding)
  ISBN-10: 0-7565-3336-8 (library binding)
1. Teapot Dome Scandal, 1921–1924—Juvenile literature.
I. Title. II. Series.
  E785.D385 2007
  973.91′4—dc22   2007004920

Visit Compass Point Books on the Internet at
www.compasspointbooks.com
or e-mail your request to
custserv@compasspointbooks.com

THE TEAPOT DOME SCANDAL

CONTENTS

A Story of Scandal

On April 14, 1922, *The Wall Street Journal* broke a disturbing story on its front page. Albert B. Fall, the U.S. secretary of the interior, had acted without government authorization to lease, or rent, government-owned oil reserves in California and Wyoming to two private business interests.

Using the words *corruption* and *scandal* to describe the incident, the article revealed that Fall had taken large amounts of bribe money to push through the leases, which would lead to millions of dollars in profit for the business interests. Because of Fall's greed, the U.S. government would lose a great deal of money to which it was entitled from the oil leases.

Fall was a powerful government official. As secretary of the interior, he had direct control

Albert Fall was a judge and senator before he became secretary of the interior.

over all public lands in the United States. He was one of President Warren G. Harding's most trusted Cabinet members, and he was a personal friend of the president as well. People began to ask questions. Did the president know about this shady deal? If he did not know about it, how could this terrible thing have happened right under his nose?

President Harding himself may not have known about Fall's dealings, but his practice of appointing friends to high government positions implicated him nevertheless. Harding and Fall's friendship

went back some years, to their first days in the U.S. Senate. When New Mexico gained statehood in 1912, Fall was elected one of its first U.S. senators. With his thick handlebar mustache and black cowboy boots, Fall seemed the perfect image of a Western state senator.

Some people thought that he looked like William F. "Buffalo Bill" Cody, the famous Wild West entertainer. Fall's life was something like a story of the Old West itself. He had been a gold miner and an Indian fighter. He had ridden with

Warren G. Harding (third from left) went on vacation with Albert Fall (left) and other friends, including Senator Joseph Frelinghuysen, Henry P. Fletcher, Albert A. Ely, and Harry M. Daugherty.

Teddy Roosevelt's Rough Riders in 1898, during the Spanish-American War. More recently, he had owned one of the largest ranches in New Mexico, where he raised beef cattle.

Soon after Fall moved to Washington, D.C., Warren Gamaliel Harding was elected as a Republican senator from Ohio. Harding arrived in the nation's capital to find that Fall's desk was right next to his in the Senate chambers. It wasn't long before Harding and the colorful senator from New Mexico became friends.

Harding was a handsome and friendly man who carried himself well. It was easy to see how he could be a politician. Harding was definitely the kind of person voters liked. He made friends wherever he went. His warm smile and firm handshake drew people to him as his political career grew. He liked being around people, and they liked being around him.

With the support of his friends and Republican Party members, Harding won the 1920 presidential election by a landslide. More than 16 million people voted for him—far more than the 10 million or so who voted for Democrat James Cox and two other minor presidential candidates. Harding entered office as one of the most popular presidents in U.S. history.

As soon as he was inaugurated on March 4, 1921, Harding rewarded the loyalty of old friends such as Fall by giving many of them influential

government roles in his administration. Harding believed that those he appointed would give him valuable advice. He thought he could count on Fall and other friends to help him in his role as president.

Warren G. Harding was the 29th president of the United States.

To Harding, the role of secretary of the interior seemed ideal for Fall. This position was traditionally held by a senator familiar with life on the frontier. Before being elected a senator from New Mexico, Fall had been a lawyer and later a judge on the

New Mexico Supreme Court. He appeared to have sound judgment and a background fit for such an esteemed role in the U.S. government.

Teapots appeared in cartoons as a symbol for the scandal, which would be known as Teapot Dome.

Soon after Harding appointed Fall, the period known as the Roaring Twenties came into full swing. A rise in economic prosperity prompted people to begin looking differently at life in general.

Many became materialists, seeking and valuing material goods such as fine clothing, jewelry, and automobiles. A "me first" attitude became common. This extended to politics and politicians. The times were ripe for a large-scale political scandal, and one had certainly been brewing.

After *The Wall Street Journal* broke the story of the leased oil reserves, details of the government corruption slowly began to emerge. It would become known as the Teapot Dome scandal, named for one of the tracts of land that Fall had secretly leased.

The Teapot Dome scandal would rock 1920s America, forcing citizens to question the role of private business interests in the public sector and to question the privileges politicians held. It marked President Harding's administration with the stain of corruption and became one of the greatest political scandals in U.S. history. ◣

A New Era

In the early 1920s, the face of politics and the voting public was changing. This change was due mostly to the effects of World War I. The war had began in Europe in 1914; the United States did not become directly involved until 1917. By the time the war ended a year later, that involvement had cost nearly 321,000 American lives.

Soldiers who survived the war returned to the United States with stories of battlefield horrors that seemed too awful to be true. Some people questioned whether the victory was worth the harsh losses. In fact, once World War I ended, people questioned many things.

Soldiers coming back from the World War I battlefields faced a world much different from the one they had left. The U.S. economy had

American soldiers fought in the trenches during World War I in Europe.

rocketed forward in the 10 years before World War I. The need for arms and food in Europe led to greater production in the United States. Once the United States entered the war, industry geared up even faster to provide ships, weapons, military clothing, and other necessities. This meant more work for everyone.

When the war ended, however, returning soldiers found that there were more people than jobs. This contributed to a slowdown in the economy. To an already disheartened population, the economic recession was an additional blow.

Many Americans felt let down, but one thing was certain: Americans wanted their lives to return to the way they had been before the United States entered the war. It was time for a change. A presidential election was coming up in 1920, and powerful politicians in the Republican Party believed they had just the man for the job—U.S. Senator Warren G. Harding.

Harding looked like many people's idea of a president, and he presented himself well. Voters from small towns and farms saw someone like themselves in Harding. He was, after all, a small-town boy from a town called Corsica, in Ohio. He had experienced first-hand the hard physical labor that was a farmer's lot.

Voters who lived in cities and toiled in factories and offices also saw Harding as a man with whom they could identify. A lifelong and loyal

Republican, Harding had been a newspaper editor before entering politics. He had been setting type for printing machines since he was a teenager, and he knew the ins and outs of a working man's life. In the minds of urban workers, Harding would make a perfect president.

Harding (fourth from left on train) campaigned in Minnesota before the 1920 presidential election.

19

The problem would come in convincing Harding he should run. As much as Harding loved his political life, he had not thought about becoming president of the United States. But Harding's old friend Harry Micajah Daugherty had a particular interest in seeing Harding become president, and Daugherty set out to change the senator's mind.

Daugherty was a business lawyer from Columbus, Ohio, who represented a number of powerful interests. His clients included railroad companies, the Armour meatpacking company, the Ohio State Telephone Company, and the American Tobacco Company. Daugherty was a shrewd judge of character. He seemed to know exactly what another person's strengths and weaknesses were, and he did not hesitate to use that knowledge to his advantage.

Like Harding, Daugherty was a skilled player in the game of politics. In Ohio, as in many other states, politicians did favors for their supporters and for other like-minded politicians. Corrupt politicians often accepted money in exchange for voting a particular way. For example, a business might make payments to a politician who

OHIO POLITICS

Ohio was one of the most politically active states. From the end of the Civil War to the end of World War I, more federal employees and Cabinet members came from the state of Ohio than anywhere else in the United States. Seven of the 12 presidents who served during that time came from Ohio, which was thought by many people to be one of the most politically corrupt states as well. If a man succeeded in Ohio politics, it was because he knew how to play the political game.

helped the business make profitable contacts. Even though this practice was fairly common, it was illegal. Politicians who accepted money tried not to get caught doing so.

Early in his career, Daugherty had been elected to the Ohio state House of Representatives. Unfortunately for Daugherty, he was accused of accepting more than $3,000 to vote as he was told.

Harry Daugherty was a shrewd politician and one of Harding's close associates.

No wrongdoing was proved, but the accusations resulted in a series of investigations, hearings, and trials. Daugherty was not convicted of a crime, but his political career had been damaged.

Not one to give up, Daugherty remained active in the Republican Party as a lobbyist, paid to influence the way politicians voted on particular issues. Lobbyists seek to influence the passage of legislation and affect government spending in certain areas. Daugherty's business and political connections made him an effective lobbyist. His enthusiasm for wheeling and dealing made him someone to be reckoned with. Many politicians recognized Daugherty's talents as an organizer and a person who got things done.

Daugherty was also known as a fixer, a person who organized corrupt deals between politicians and others. He did not hold political office, but as a lobbyist and a fixer, Daugherty spent a great deal of time with government officials. It

FIXERS

People who knew how to use bribes and favors to fix things for others were known as fixers. Perhaps an individual wanted to make sure that his son-in-law was appointed to a county government job. That individual could pay money to a fixer to help that job come through. The fixer would, in turn, talk to his friends in government and maybe pass on to his government friend a little of the money he had received. His political friend would then talk to yet another person to make sure the government job went to the right person. Fixers relied on this complicated system of money bribes and favors owed to accomplish what they wanted in business and government.

would be to Daugherty's benefit, and the benefit of the people who worked with him, to have a high-placed political friend. If Harding were to become president, Daugherty would have the highest-placed political friend in the United States.

Other powerful leaders in the Republican Party also supported Harding's candidacy. William Harrison Hays, the chairman of the Republican National Committee, supported Harding and spearheaded his presidential campaign.

Powerful figures in the Republican Party supported Harding at the Republican National Convention of 1920.

23

In addition, several political bosses endorsed Harding. In each state, political bosses had a great deal of control over who was nominated for and elected to office. These bosses usually did not hold office themselves but used other, often illegal, means to control politicians. For example, they might pay money to a politician to vote a particular way or do the politician a favor. One of the most important of these bosses was Boise Penrose of Pennsylvania. He was considered to be the bosses' boss. No one was more powerful than Penrose. He sent word to his followers at the Republican National Convention that Harding was his choice for the nomination.

With Harding as president, the political bosses and their friends would have a great deal of influence over national policies. This influence could, in some cases, mean the opportunity to make a lot of money. For example, Prohibition was in full swing. Pharmacies needed a special license to sell medicinal drugs and alcohol. Although only a limited number of licenses were available, for the right price a person in the right political office could make sure a license was issued. The practice was illegal, but it was profitable.

Not all politicians were under the influence of the bosses, of course. For them, Harding presented the stable image that the American voters wanted. He would be good for the country. He seemed to be just the right type of leader to help the nation return to the good old days before

the war had changed everything. Harding seemed to be a good choice all the way around.

Federal agents captured illegal alcohol during Prohibition, which lasted from 1920 until 1933.

Many of Harding's speeches contained a soothing promise to voters: There would be a return to normal times. Harding used the word *normalcy* to describe the return to a peaceful and happier United States. He said:

> *America's present need is not heroics but healing, not nostrums [remedies] but normalcy.*

American voters believed Harding, and he easily won the 1920 presidential election. ▧

The President's Friends

When President Harding moved into the White House, one of the first things he did was to open up parts of the mansion to the public. This was just the opposite of what the previous president, Woodrow Wilson, had done. Whereas Wilson was very private about the running of the government, Harding appeared to have no secrets.

It was not unusual for Harding to come out to greet the ordinary citizens who had voted him into office. He warmly welcomed them to the White House, and hosted many prominent people of the early 1920s. Harding made the voters feel they had made the right choice for president. They trusted President Harding, and they trusted that he would choose a Cabinet worthy of the American people.

Harding welcomed many people to the White House, including physicist Marie Curie (third from left) in May 1921.

Soon after he was elected, Harding appointed Harry Daugherty as attorney general in gratitude for his help during the presidential election campaign. Although Harding was acting as a loyal friend, he was not necessarily acting as a responsible leader. Daugherty's appointment was the first of Harding's several mistakes in choosing his advisers.

Harding spent much of his time between his election in November 1920 and his inauguration in March 1921 selecting his new Cabinet, as depicted in cartoons from the time.

Harding appointed another friend, New Mexico Senator Albert B. Fall, as secretary of the interior. Harding may have counted Fall as a friend, but that was not how most other politicians viewed him. Like Daugherty, Fall had an unsavory reputation.

ONCE OVER THIS OBSTACLE AND IT LOOKS LIKE FAIR GOING

CABINET BUNKER

Before Fall's election to the Senate, he had acted as a defense attorney for two men accused of murdering Colonel Albert Jennings Fountain and his young son, Henry. Fall managed to win acquittals for his clients. The problem was that Fall was a landowner, and Fountain just happened to be one of his biggest rivals. Fall and Fountain were enemies.

Colonel Fountain had often challenged Fall's tactics in trying to get as much land as possible. One of these tactics was the use of gunmen to scare local residents into selling their land. Fountain believed

WARREN G. HARDING'S CABINET	
Secretary of War	John W. Weeks
Secretary of the Navy	Edwin C. Denby
Secretary of the Interior	Albert B. Fall
Attorney General	Harry M. Daugherty
Secretary of Agriculture	Henry Wallace
Secretary of Labor	James Davis
Postmaster General	William Hays
Secretary of the Treasury	Andrew W. Mellon
Secretary of Commerce	Herbert Hoover
Secretary of State	Charles Evans Hughes

Fall was as crooked as they came. Fall saw Fountain as an obstacle to owning even bigger ranches in New Mexico than he already had.

Since the bodies of Fountain and his son were never found, Fall was able to secure the freedom of the accused killers. Although Fall was never directly linked to the murders of Fountain and his son, the suspicion of his involvement stayed with him throughout his political career. But Harding ignored this suspicion and those who were against Fall's appointment. Fall joined the Cabinet.

To fill the role of postmaster general of the United States, Harding turned to William Hays, the chairman of the Republican National Committee

President Warren G. Harding (third from right in front) posed with Vice President Calvin Coolidge (second from right in front) and members of his Cabinet on the White House lawn early in his administration.

who had spearheaded Harding's presidential campaign. As postmaster general, Hays controlled thousands of jobs. These jobs were typically considered patronage jobs. In the patronage system, politicians reward loyal supporters with jobs.

During the administration of Harding's predecessor, Woodrow Wilson, 13,000 patronage jobs were transferred out of the control of the postmaster general's office. After Harding appointed Hays to the position, Harding transferred those jobs right back. By doing this, Harding sent a message to the voters that his administration would practice favoritism in political jobs. To some newspaper editors, it seemed that Harding was opening the doors to political corruption as well.

Harding appointed Edwin C. Denby to the position of secretary of the Navy. This gave Denby control over all oil reserves, land, military equipment, and everything else assigned to the U.S. Navy. Denby was a self-made millionaire. He had made his fortune in the automobile business in Detroit, Michigan. He was also a lawyer and had been elected to the U.S. House of Representatives in 1904. Denby was a loyal Republican who had served in the Marines during World War I.

Edwin Denby brought World War I military experience to his appointment as secretary of the Navy.

John W. Weeks was appointed Harding's secretary of war. Among other things, this gave Weeks control of surplus military supplies from World War I. It also gave him the authority to plan and construct hospitals for the many veterans of the war. Weeks transferred the responsibility for these two undertakings to the new head of the Veterans' Bureau, Charles Forbes. Although Forbes was not an official Cabinet member, he was a good friend of Harding's.

Some people were critical of the individuals Harding selected for his Cabinet. Bruce Bliven, a newspaper editor in the early 1920s, said that Harding had appointed to his Cabinet "one of the most astonishing collections of crooks, grafters, and blackmailers ever assembled." The group of appointees and their associates that Bliven was referring to became known as the Ohio Gang.

THE OHIO GANG

Harding's political appointees, known as the Ohio Gang, included Harding's friends such as Harry Daugherty, Charles Forbes, and Albert Fall. They were considered by many to be particularly talented crooks who used their positions for a great deal of personal gain. Instead of advising Harding on how to best be president, most of the Ohio Gang betrayed Harding and the public by their involvement in shady political deals, graft, and bribery. Although called the Ohio Gang, most of the members were not native to the state of Ohio. Daugherty was from Ohio, while Forbes and Fall were not. Because of the activities of the Ohio Gang, the Harding administration is considered to be one of the most corrupt in the history of the presidency.

Public Resources, Private Profits

Early in the decade before Harding's presidency, concerns were growing that a great war was on the horizon. In 1912, President William Howard Taft used information gathered by the Public Lands Commission to withdraw certain oil reserves from public land use and set them aside for the exclusive use of the U.S. Navy. The Naval Oil Reserves were 70,000 acres (28,000 hectares) of federally owned oil lands in Elk Hills and Buena Vista, California, and in Salt Creek, Wyoming. The Wyoming reserve was known as Teapot Dome. It was named after a rock structure on the land that was shaped like a teapot and called Teapot Rock.

To most people, it only made sense that oil intended for use by Navy warships should be under the control of the Navy. On June 4, 1920,

The Teapot Dome oil fields got their name from Teapot Rock, a rock structure that was approximately 75 feet (22.5 meters) high and featured a spout.

THE PUBLIC LANDS COMMISSION

Between 1879 and 1903, Congress had directed a special group of people to identify lands that were supposed to be owned by the government. This group, the Public Lands Commission, reported on how the lands were being used. The first reports were submitted throughout 1880 and 1881. Even though the commission had specific ideas on how the land and its resources might be preserved, the ideas were largely ignored. By the time the second Public Lands Commission was established in 1903, many public resources had become endangered. With World War I on the horizon, the idea of a shortage of oil resources caused a great deal of concern and led to the creation of the Naval Oil Reserves.

Congress passed a bill that gave the secretary of the Navy control over the oil reserves. The bill read:

> *[The secretary may] conserve, develop, use and operate the same in his discretion, directly or by contract, lease, or otherwise, and to use, store, exchange or sell the oil and gas products thereof, and those from all royalty oil from lands in the naval reserves, for the benefit of the United States.*

At the end of World War I and after Harding took office, the oil reserves were still available. The Navy had not used the reserves, but they were available should the Department of the Navy need them. Secretary of the Interior Fall, however, had an idea how those oil resources should be used. His idea did not include the Navy.

Like Fall, many Westerners felt that lands and public resources such as coal and oil should be made available to private business interests. As a private rancher and businessman, Fall depended on vast tracts of public land to graze his cattle. Fall was part of a segment of the American public who believed that private businesses should be allowed to develop the land and use the resources to make a profit.

The Naval Oil Reserves were established in the Western states of Wyoming and California.

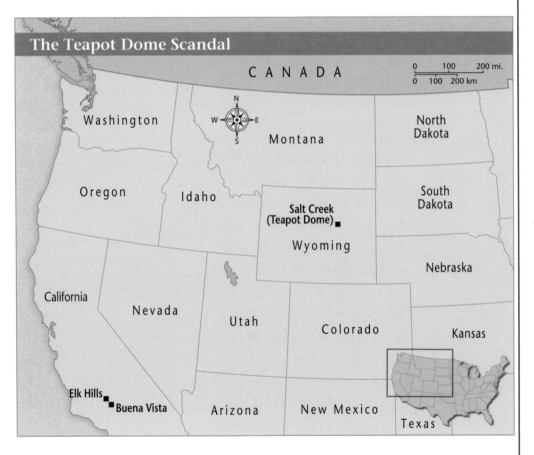

The Teapot Dome Scandal

At the same time, though, these businesses would pay a portion of those profits to the government. Supporters of this idea believed that the more businesses profited, the more the U.S. government profited—and, in turn, so did all Americans. The people in favor of allowing private development of public resources felt that there was an abundance of resources there for the taking and that these resources were not likely to run out for many hundreds of years—if ever.

Other Americans, however, did not see the connection between private use of public land and a benefit to the average citizen. Then, as now, people questioned how public resources such as oil and coal could best be used. Some politicians and voter groups felt that all public resources belonged to the American people and should be protected from use by private businesses. The people who took this view felt that there was a limited amount of available oil, coal,

WHO OWNED WHAT?

Until the late 19th century, there was no real government control over how the country's rich resources were used. As settlement spread westward, individuals and businesses bought huge tracts of land with acres and acres of standing timber. These individuals claimed all the resources and the right to use those resources for their own profit. Even lands that were supposed to be set aside for public use were sometimes used for profit by private individuals. There was real confusion regarding the laws that controlled public lands and how those lands should be used for the benefit of the American people as a whole.

and other resources. If businesses were allowed to use these resources without government control of their activities, the resources would run out within a short amount of time.

Albert Fall, of course, disagreed with this view. As secretary of the interior, he now had control of all public lands in the United States. His job was to ensure that they were put to good use. Fall wanted to add the oil reserves to those public lands under his control.

Soon after he was appointed to his Cabinet post, Fall told President Harding that private businesses drilling close to the federal reserves were possibly draining off some of the reserve oil.

He had the perfect solution to the problem: Transfer control of the oil reserves from the Department of the Navy to the Department of the Interior—his department. Fall pointed out that his department would protect the oil reserves better than the Navy could, because the Department of the Interior controlled all public lands.

Furthermore, Fall himself had direct experience with the oil-drilling industry in his home state of New Mexico. Who better to oversee the public's interest than a government official with knowledge of oil and how best to use it? Fall even convinced the secretary of the Navy, Edwin Denby, to support the transfer of control of the Naval Oil Reserves.

Fall's argument contained some truth. Private drilling operations could, indeed, drain off some of the oil from the reserve land. However, Fall supported the idea that businesses should be able to develop public resources. His support of private business interests on public lands did not make him the best candidate to be the protector of public lands or of public resources such as coal and oil.

One of Fall's main opponents on the issue was Senator Robert La Follette of Wisconsin. The Republican senator publicly protested the proposed move of the federal oil reserves to the Department of the Interior, and he tried to motivate other senators to block it. His efforts, however, failed.

President Harding trusted Fall and believed Fall's arguments about protecting the oil reserves from unlawful drilling. On May 31, 1921, Harding signed Executive Order Number 3474, transferring control of the oil reserves to the Department of the Interior.

ROBERT LA FOLLETTE

Robert La Follette served as a Republican in the U.S. House of Representatives from 1885 to 1891. In 1900, he was elected governor of Wisconsin. In 1905, La Follette was elected to the U.S. Senate, where he served until his death in 1925. Throughout his political career, La Follette fought the power of the official leadership of the Republican Party, which he thought was corrupt. He was also a reformer and worked hard to pass laws that regulated the railroad industry. He fought against the political power of big business, which he believed had too much influence on political decisions.

Fall, however, was facing financial hardship. His ranches were not producing enough money, and he had already borrowed funds to help keep them running. Fall was heavily in debt, and circumstances were ripe for him to give in to temptation and accept a bribe to work with private businesses to develop the oil resources.

Senator Robert La Follette, also known as "Fighting Bob," has been called the conscience of the Republican Party. His portrait hangs in the Capitol as one of the five most outstanding senators in U.S. history.

Fall did not waste time planning his next move. By the last months of 1921, Fall had already made the first contacts with certain private businessmen to discuss profitable, and secret, leases on the oil reserves.

One of Fall's contacts was Edward L. Doheny, the owner of the Pan American Petroleum and Transport Company. He had been a longtime friend of Albert Fall's. As young men, Fall had met Doheny while working around the mines of Silver City, New Mexico. Fall had entered politics and the cattle business. Doheny went into the oil business and became extremely wealthy. He was very interested in getting his hands on the oil reserves.

Doheny had made millions of dollars during his career, but Fall had met with harder times. Doheny was only too willing to help his friend. In November 1921, he loaned Fall $100,000. Fall did not have to pay interest on this loan, and there was no specific date by which the loan had to be paid back.

In 1922, Fall returned the favor by giving Doheny the rights to drill for oil at the oil reserves in Elk Hills and Buena Vista, California. The secret lease agreement Doheny signed with Fall and the Department of the Interior called for Doheny's company to build, at its own expense, storage tanks and a pipeline for the U.S. government. This agreement was just fine with Doheny. He said, "We will be in bad luck if we do not get $100 million in profit." Compared to that huge amount of money, the cost of building the pipeline and tanks was very small.

Fall did not stop at the secret lease with Doheny. While Fall negotiated with his old friend, he was also negotiating with Harry Ford Sinclair, another wealthy businessman, to lease yet another reserve.

Sinclair was worth even more money than Doheny. Sinclair owned the Sinclair Oil Company, a huge and very profitable business. Fall received $400,000 from Sinclair, who also

Edward L. Doheny was the millionaire owner of an oil company and Fall's close friend, which put him in a good position to make a profit from government-owned oil resources.

Harry Ford Sinclair was a wealthy oil company owner who hoped to profit from his association with Fall.

sent expensive livestock to Fall's ranch in New Mexico. For these favors, Fall leased the oil reserves at Teapot Dome, Wyoming, to Sinclair. Like Doheny, Sinclair was to build storage tanks and pipelines and fill them with fuel oil, or oil that has been refined and is ready to be used. The oil Sinclair would be drilling in the reserves was crude, or unrefined, oil. Sinclair would have to bear the cost of refining the oil that would

OIL BARON

Harry Ford Sinclair started his career as a pharmacist in Kansas. When an opportunity came up in 1901 to own a part of the White Oil Company, Sinclair took it. By 1916, he knew he had found his calling. He formed Sinclair Oil by combining 11 smaller petroleum companies. By the end of the 1920s, Sinclair's refineries were processing 80,000 barrels a day. His company had also built almost 900 miles (1,440 kilometers) of oil pipelines.

be stored in the government's tanks. With this arrangement, Sinclair expected to make at least $100 million. Having control of the oil reserves was proving to be a wonderful opportunity for Fall to get out of debt.

Front Page News

Even though Fall tried to conceal the lease agreements he had made, some of the details began to leak out. Fall's neighbors in New Mexico noticed that he suddenly had the money to buy more ranchland and to pay off old debts. Oilmen in Wyoming and California alerted their congressmen about their new neighbors, Doheny and Sinclair.

People started to ask all kinds of questions. Why had Doheny and Sinclair been awarded the leases to the oil reserves? If the oil reserves were to be leased to private interests, why hadn't they been put up for bid to any oil business that was interested? Shouldn't the leases be awarded to the oil company or business that offered the best deal to the government? All of these considerations had been bypassed with Fall's

Drilling for oil was big business for the U.S. government as well as private owners.

secret contracts. People speculated that Fall had cheated the government out of millions of dollars in revenue from the oil leases. Then the newspapers got wind of the story.

The Wall Street Journal broke the story of the secret oil leases on April 14, 1922, revealing that Albert Fall had taken large amounts of bribe money to push through the leases. Because the public had so much confidence in President Harding, however, most Americans did not pay much attention to the story. They could not accept that his administration would have anything to do with bribery, corruption, and scandal.

Some senators and newspaper reporters, though, had long held doubts about Harding's administration. While the American people saw only the trustworthy image of President Harding, many politicians in Washington, D.C., recognized that several of Harding's closest advisers were crooks. Now it seemed that Harding would be forced to acknowledge the truth.

Senator La Follette led the movement to investigate Fall's actions. La Follette spoke to other senators and to the press. He gained support, and the Senate responded to the disturbing questions being asked by passing Resolution 277 on April 15, 1922. This resolution asked Secretary of the Navy Edwin Denby and Secretary of the Interior Albert Fall to inform the Senate whether leases had been given on the oil reserves. If leases had been given to certain people or businesses, the Senate wanted to know the names of the leaseholders and the terms of the lease agreements.

Fall was out of town when Resolution 277 was passed, so he could not directly respond to the Senate's questions. Edward Finney was the acting secretary of the interior during Fall's absence. Finney and Edwin Denby gave a copy of the leases to the Senate, along with a letter defending the lease agreements that had been signed.

The agreement to allow Doheny and Sinclair to take crude oil out of the reserves was in the U.S. government's best interests, Finney and Denby wrote. The leases allowed for the exchange of crude oil for refined oil that the Navy could use.

Newspapers were quick to respond to the news of Fall's profitable secret lease of the reserve at Teapot Dome. Political cartoons often featured a steaming teapot.

The leases also allowed for the storage of that refined oil. Denby and Finney said that the leases did not violate any government policy.

After reviewing the leases, however, the senators disagreed with Denby's opinion. The Senate passed Resolution 282 on April 29, 1922. That action provided for a special investigation into the lease agreements. The investigation would be under the control of the Committee of Public Lands and Surveys. Senator Thomas Walsh, a Democrat from Montana, headed the committee. Walsh was a lawyer and had been a U.S. senator since 1912.

Even as the Senate announced its investigation, other oil industry members let it be known that they were outraged at Fall's secret lease negotiations. It was obvious to them that Fall seemed to have come into a lot of money very quickly. Where had it come from?

These members of the oil industry complained that there was no state of emergency that required that the naval reserves be opened for anyone to use, much less private oil companies that stood to make a profit. A large reserve of oil stored in above-ground tanks and pipelines already existed. In fact, the current stored amount of oil was greater than ever before. There was an abundant supply of oil, and the prices for refined oil were low. There was plenty of refined oil for the Navy—or anyone else—to use without tapping into the oil reserves in California and at Teapot Dome.

Thomas Walsh was a prosecutor before he was elected a senator.

Members of the oil industry also pointed out that the oil industry itself was just coming out of the worst economic depression it had ever experienced. The industry made money by pumping out crude oil, refining it, and then selling it as fuel in the marketplace. Fall's private lease agreement with Doheny and Sinclair enabled them to drive the price of crude oil even lower while the price of refined oil remained the same. Doheny and Sinclair stood to make a huge profit while the people buying the fuel oil continued to pay the same price. The oil buyers saw no savings.

Members of the oil industry funneled their objections through Senator Robert La Follette. The oil industry representatives sent Senator La Follette a letter, which he presented on the Senate floor on May 13, 1922. The letter outlined three areas of protest:

> *First. Against the policy of the secretary of the interior and the secretary of the Navy in opening the naval reserves at this time for exploitation.*
>
> *Second. Against the method of leasing public lands without competitive bidding, as exemplified in the recent contract entered into between Secretary Fall of the Interior and Secretary Denby of the Navy and the Standard Oil-Sinclair-Doheny interest.*
>
> *Third. Against the policy of any department of the government of the United States entering into a contract of any character whatsoever, whether competitive or not, which would tend to continue or perpetuate a monopolistic control of the oil industry of the United States or create a monopoly on the sale of fuel oil or refined oil to the Navy or any other department of the government.*

By now, President Harding was also hearing rumblings about Fall's dealings. Harding did not want to believe that his friend would be involved in any criminal activity. Harding sent a letter to the Senate:

The policy which has been adopted by the Secretary of the Navy and the Secretary of the Interior in dealing with these matters was submitted to me prior to the adoption thereof, and the policy decided upon and the subsequent acts have at all times had my entire approval.

One of President Harding's dogs greeted him and the first lady, Florence Harding, on their return from a trip to Florida.

53

Privately, however, Harding was worried. He did not know all the details of Fall's activities, and he was concerned that the man he had trusted had done something that would prove to be a serious offense. If the accusations were true, Harding's reputation would suffer.

Harding's worries over the oil reserve leases worsened his already failing health. The once lively and outgoing president appeared increasingly frail throughout 1922. In 1923, Harding began a cross-country tour that would take him to Alaska. Even as he once again met with adoring crowds of citizens, Harding was heartsick at the thought of a possible scandal. He expressed his fears to a companion:

> *My God, this is a hell of a job! I have no trouble with my enemies. I can take care of them. But my friends, my goddamned friends, they're the ones that keep me walking the floor at nights.*

Harding made it clear to those around him that he felt he was being betrayed by men he believed were friends as well as advisers. No one knows for sure how much Harding actually knew about Fall's doings, because tragedy struck before all of Fall's activities came to light. Although he had been treated for heart trouble and pneumonia, Harding appeared to be recovering when he died unexpectedly on August 2, 1923, in San Francisco, California.

FAREWELL TO A PRESIDENT

After President Warren G. Harding died, his body traveled by train from California to Washington, D.C., where it lay in state. The train moved east at a snail's pace. Thousands of men, women, and children lined the railroad tracks. Over and over again, people along the train's route sang Harding's favorite hymn, "Lead, Kindly Knight." One reporter for *The New York Times* wrote that the expression of national grief was believed to be "the most remarkable demonstration in American history of affection, respect, and reverence for the dead." At the time, the Teapot Dome scandal was only a whisper in the news, and Harding had a reputation as a great-hearted individual and a noble president.

With Harding's death, Vice President Calvin Coolidge assumed the presidency—as well as the responsibility of finding out what had really happened with the oil reserve leases. ◤

The Investigation Begins

Chapter

6

On October 15, 1923, the Senate Committee on Public Lands and Surveys began hearings on the California and Teapot Dome oil leases. But only three members of the nine–person committee showed up. By law, a quorum, or a majority of the committee members, was required in order to proceed with the meeting. Because there was not a quorum, the meeting was rescheduled for the following week.

The committee was headed by a Democrat, Senator Thomas Walsh of Montana. It included both Democratic and Republican members, in an effort to ensure that the investigation would be carried out fairly. The possible scandal had taken place during a Republican administration, and the government officials under suspicion were also Republicans. As a result, some Republican

politicians felt that the whole investigation was just an effort on the part of Democrats to cause trouble. Everyone soon learned, though, that the trouble had already started, and it had little to do with one political party or the other.

On October 23, 1923, the first key witness was called before the committee. The witness was Albert B. Fall, now the former secretary of the interior, having resigned from his position earlier that year. From the very beginning of his testimony, Fall refused to provide the committee with any details concerning the leases he had signed.

The Senate Committee on Public Lands and Surveys, headed by Senator Thomas J. Walsh (second from left), was appointed to investigate the Teapot Dome oil scandal.

Albert Fall resigned as secretary of the interior in March 1923.

He claimed that the situation surrounding the leases was a matter of national security. If he were to make the details public, enemies of the United States would know the government's plans concerning oil production. Fall said he did not want the country's enemies to think that the United States was strengthening its Navy by storing large quantities of oil. When asked why he had not put the leases out for bid so that a number of oil companies could bid on them, Fall claimed that he knew he could get a better price for the oil without the bidding process. Again, he cited national security.

The committee members rejected Fall's defense and asked once again for an explanation. Fall refused to provide it. Fall acted as if he were in a court of law and refused to say anything that might have been viewed as an admission that he had done something illegal. Fall invoked the Fifth Amendment to the U.S. Constitution, which states in part that a person cannot be forced to testify against himself or herself in a court of law. Even though the committee investigation was not a proceeding in a court of law, Fall refused to say anything that might have been viewed as an admission of guilt.

The committee members were getting little information from Fall, so they next called Secretary of the Navy Edwin Denby to testify. Denby simply repeated what he had already told the Senate. He was aware of the leases, and they were perfectly acceptable to the Navy. He was not aware of any special deals that Fall might have made with Doheny or Sinclair. Denby himself did not ask for, or receive, any kind of bribe in exchange for agreeing to the lease. Senator Walsh, however, was convinced there was more to the story than Denby and Fall were acknowledging. The problem was finding the proof.

PLEADING THE FIFTH

The Fifth Amendment to the U.S. Constitution offers a particular type of protection. It states that individuals under oath in a courtroom cannot be forced to testify against themselves. If a person on a witness stand believes that answering certain questions would unfairly point the finger of guilt, the suspect can call on the Fifth Amendment for the right to refuse to answer. Although the Fifth Amendment might seem to hand criminals a free pass out of court, the amendment is intended to prevent members of the court from using intimidation or force to make a suspect falsely admit guilt.

Early in the Teapot Dome investigation, Secretary of the Navy Edwin Denby announced to reporters that he would not resign from his post.

From October 1923 through May 1924, the Senate Committee on Public Lands and Surveys called on dozens of witnesses to testify. The committee members wanted to prove that Fall had taken bribes to award the leases to Doheny and Sinclair. Week after week passed, and witness after witness spoke

before the committee. The investigation seemed to lose its momentum. The committee simply did not yet have the evidence it needed to bring Fall, and whoever else was involved, to justice.

During this time, Walsh pursued every possible lead he could. He knew that Fall had obtained a large amount of money from somewhere. Shortly after the leases were signed, Fall had managed to pay the government several years of back taxes. He had also made expensive improvements to his New Mexico ranches. Where had this money come from? Walsh tried to track down the source.

Some members of the press and rival politicians called Walsh a scandalmonger, a person who tries to dig up distasteful information about other people's private lives. President Harding still had many supporters, even after his death. They did not want his presidency tainted with a possible scandal. Walsh's phones were tapped, and he received anonymous letters threatening his life if he did not stop the investigation. Despite the risks, Walsh continued with the task he'd been given.

In January 1924, Walsh finally got the breakthrough he had been looking for. Evidence came to light about what Fall had received as part of the lease agreements with Doheny and Sinclair.

Archie Roosevelt, the son of former President Theodore Roosevelt and the brother of Assistant Secretary of the Navy Theodore Roosevelt II, had worked as an executive in Harry Sinclair's company when Fall signed the lease agreements. On January 24, 1924, he testified that he had been told a curious story by Sinclair's private secretary, G.D. Wahlberg. According to Wahlberg, Sinclair had paid $68,000 to Fall's New Mexico ranch manager. Roosevelt found this very suspicious. He had a feeling that something underhanded was going on. Because of this, Roosevelt resigned his position.

When Wahlberg was called by the committee to testify, he denied saying any such thing. What he claimed he had actually said was that the $68,000 was not intended for Fall's ranch manager but for Sinclair's horse farm manager. Sinclair owned a famous thoroughbred horse racing stable. The money was to be paid there, not to Fall's ranch, Wahlberg said.

The committee did not believe Wahlberg, especially since Sinclair had decided that he had urgent business in Europe at the same time the committee was holding its hearings. Roosevelt had informed the committee that there was no such business that would require Sinclair's presence. Sinclair was obviously trying to avoid having to testify before Walsh and the other eight committee members.

That same day—January 24, 1924— Albert Fall's longtime friend and the head of the Pan American Petroleum and Transport Company, Edward Doheny, testified before the committee.

Doheny admitted to the committee that he had lent Fall $100,000. Doheny's son had brought the cash to Fall at his ranch. Doheny swore that the money was not a bribe but a loan.

Archie Roosevelt's testimony about suspicious activity at Sinclair Oil made him an important witness during the investigation of the Teapot Dome scandal.

63

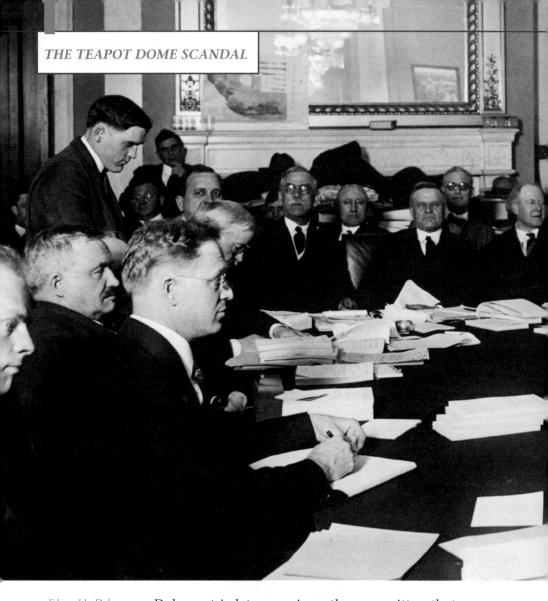

Edward L. Doheny (second from right at the table) testified before the Senate committee investigating the Teapot Dome oil leases.

Doheny tried to convince the committee that $100,000 wasn't enough to be considered a bribe. Doheny was so wealthy that $100,000 was a very small sum to him. He told the committee that it was "no more than $25 or $50 to the ordinary individual." The committee disagreed. The next steps that the government took led to a special prosecution that was the first of its kind in U.S. history.

While several previous presidents had appointed special prosecutors, none of them had been subject to approval by or in any way under the eye of the U.S. Senate. The Teapot Dome investigation would become the first instance in which special prosecutors were appointed by the president—with the advice and consent of the Senate—to investigate wrongdoing by government officials.

Special Prosecutors

On Saturday, January 26, 1924, Senator Walsh told the committee that he would present a special resolution to the U.S. Senate on the following Monday. The resolution would request that President Coolidge make invalid the California and Teapot Dome oil leases Fall had signed with Doheny and Sinclair. The resolution would also ask Coolidge to appoint special lawyers to further investigate the matter and prosecute anyone who had been involved in setting up the leases. Everyone on the committee agreed with Walsh's proposal.

Coolidge, however, acted before Walsh had a chance to introduce the resolution. At midnight that night, the president made a statement that would appear in Sunday's newspapers. He said that he would appoint two special lawyers to handle the Teapot Dome case.

Coolidge's statement began:

> *It is not for the president to determine criminal guilt or render judgment in civil causes. That is the function of the courts. It is not for him to prejudge. I shall do neither; but when facts are revealed to me that require action for the purpose of insuring the enforcement of either civil or criminal liability, such action will be taken. That is the province of the executive.*

Coolidge had a sticky problem, though. Which lawyers should he appoint? If he appointed Republicans, then the Democrats would say that the investigation would be nothing more than a cover-up—Republicans protecting other Republicans. If Coolidge appointed Democrats, then the Republicans might protest by saying that the Democrats could not be counted on to be fair in their investigations of key Republican government officials, such as Fall and Denby.

President Coolidge recognized that if the accusations were true, the scandal would reflect very poorly on everyone at the highest reaches of government. Even though Coolidge had nothing to do with the situation, the question would always remain about whether Harding had known of all the double-dealing and bribery of which Fall and other Cabinet members were suspected. The whole situation would be a shameful embarrassment. Even so, Coolidge sent an important message to the American public when he said:

> *I feel the public is entitled to know that in the conduct of such action, no one is shielded for any party, political, or other reason.*

Coolidge's solution was to appoint two special lawyers, a Republican and a Democrat.

In most cases, the responsibility for investigating a government bribery case would fall to the attorney general. However, Harry Daugherty had been less than helpful during the committee proceedings. Congressional approval of Coolidge's plan was gained because members of Congress had no confidence in Attorney General Daugherty. In truth, the appointment of two lawyers who didn't work for Daugherty's Justice Department made it clear that neither the president nor other politicians believed that Daugherty was totally innocent.

President Coolidges's first two choices for the special lawyers were Republican Silas Strawn and Democrat Thomas Gregory. Both were able lawyers, but both also had connections to the oil industry. The Senate would have to approve of the two lawyers selected to prosecute the case, and Strawn's and Gregory's links to the oil business would be enough to prevent their approval.

Although Attorney General Daugherty had been President Harding's close friend, he was not trusted by many people in the government.

So Coolidge turned to Owen Roberts, a Republican from Pennsylvania, and Atlee Pomerene, a Democrat and former senator from Ohio. The president made it clear that it was very important that the two lawyers put aside any party loyalty. As they investigated this case, they had to forget that they were Republican or Democrat. Coolidge said to Roberts:

> *If you are confirmed, there is one thing you must bear in mind. You will be working for the government of the United States—not for the Republican Party, and not for me. Let this fact guide you, no matter what ugly matters come to light.*

On February 16, 1924, the U.S. Senate confirmed the appointment of both Pomerene and Roberts. Driven by public criticism, Edwin Denby resigned as secretary of the Navy on February 18. The criminal investigation into the Teapot Dome scandal was under way.

One of the first stops for the special lawyers was a visit with Senator Walsh. The senator had spent 18 months investigating the oil leases and possible bribes involving Fall, Doheny, and Sinclair. During that time, Walsh had pulled together information that would be useful to Roberts and Pomerene.

The first bit of information Walsh shared was about Attorney General Daugherty, whom he considered untrustworthy. Walsh said to them:

I wouldn't depend on the Justice Department for investigative purposes, nor would I approach the Attorney General's office for information if I were you. … It is my conviction that the man would go to any lengths to protect himself and his friends—and make no mistake about it, the people we are after are friends of the Attorney General. Harry Daugherty has had a hand in every dirty piece of business which has come out of the Harding administration. There is every reason to believe that, at the very least, Daugherty is one of the men who knows the whole sordid story of the oil leases—and there is enough evidence to warrant the suspicion that he himself might have profited from them. In addition, the Department of Justice and its Bureau of Investigation are handpicked by Daugherty and rotten to the core.

After months of work tracking down information on the oil leases, Senator Thomas J. Walsh was in a unique position to advise Atlee Pomerene and Owen Roberts.

Walsh's poor opinion of Daugherty was echoed throughout Congress and in the newspapers of the day. It was more than just a case of one political figure disliking and distrusting another. Daugherty's long history of double-dealing and dishonesty was beginning to catch up to him. Throughout the committee investigation, those following the hearings asked why Daugherty as attorney general was not trying to prosecute Fall.

Daugherty defended his lack of action by saying that he did not feel that it was appropriate that he investigate Fall, a fellow Cabinet member in the Harding administration. According to Daugherty, he had spoken to Coolidge about the oil field leases and suggested that Coolidge appoint lawyers outside the Justice Department. Daugherty's reputation was so poor, however, that few people believed he had done anything of the sort.

Public mistrust of Daugherty grew because he had repeatedly turned a blind eye to corruption within Harding's administration. For example, Daugherty had ignored corrupt deals undertaken by Veterans' Bureau head Charles Forbes, who sold off Army surplus materials for a profit. Forbes had also given contracts to construction companies to build hospitals. The contractors who got the work were those who had given Forbes the biggest bribes. It is estimated that in just under two years, more than $200 million of government money went to graft and wasteful purchases made by Forbes' department. These purchases included $70,000 in floor cleaner and floor wax!

Despite this obvious corruption, Daugherty did not believe that such matters warranted prosecution by his office. As attorney general, Daugherty should have prosecuted Forbes and the many others like him within the Harding administration. Daugherty's failure to act pointed to his knowledge and possible involvement with the shady deals that had been going on for years.

The Senate made its distrust of Daugherty and the Justice Department a matter of public record. Senator Burton Wheeler of Montana introduced Senate Resolution 157. In it, he asked for an investigation of the Justice Department and of Attorney General Daugherty. Wheeler took the floor of the Senate and said:

> *Ever since the attorney general has occupied the important position which he now holds, various charges have been made against him in the newspapers and by individuals from one end of the country to the other. Recently, when the oil scandal first developed, it appears that the attorney general's name was mixed in it. ... Everybody knows he was the friend of Sinclair. Everybody knows that he was the friend of Doheny.*

Wheeler then went on to point out other instances of corruption in which Daugherty and the office of the attorney general were involved. Daugherty strongly denied Wheeler's accusations. He said that he had never acted upon any information that resulted in his personal profit. He also said that Fall had not asked for his opinion concerning the oil leases, so Daugherty did not offer his opinion. Daugherty said, "I had no part of any kind ... directly or indirectly, in the negotiations leading up to the execution of the oil leases." Despite Daugherty's claims of innocence, the Senate passed Resolution 157 by a vote of 66 to 1. Daugherty still fought to keep his position as attorney general. However, Coolidge pressured him to resign, which Daugherty did on March 28, 1924.

The overwhelming vote in favor of Senate Resolution 157 reinforced the importance of the appointment of the two special prosecution lawyers. Pomerene and Roberts quickly got to work. They first reviewed all of the records put together by the U.S. Senate during the previous years of investigation. They looked closely at the complaints the investigating committee had filed against both Doheny's and Sinclair's oil companies. Their next step was to hire private detectives and send them to New York, California, New Mexico, and Texas—states where Doheny and Sinclair lived and conducted most of their business. The detectives were looking for evidence that Fall had taken bribes to assign the oil leases to Doheny and Sinclair.

U.S. Senator Burton K. Wheeler was the voice of the Senate in asking for an investigation into the shady activities of Attorney General Harry Daugherty.

75

Secret Service Agent Thomas B. Foster was assigned the task of carefully reviewing Albert Fall's financial records. While working in Colorado, Foster returned to his hotel room one night to find that it had been broken into and ransacked. Despite the danger, the special prosecutors' team kept looking for the evidence it needed, and traveled to Canada, Cuba, and France in search of witnesses.

As soon as they had enough evidence, Roberts and Pomerene began to bring the cases to court. They filed several different types of lawsuits. The special prosecutors were trying to get the oil leases canceled and the oil reserves returned to the government. They were also trying to get convictions against Fall, Doheny, and Sinclair for defrauding, or cheating, the U.S. government.

On March 13, 1924, they filed a lawsuit against Sinclair's Mammoth Oil Company, a company that Sinclair had created to operate the Teapot Dome fields, to cancel the Teapot Dome lease. Sinclair used his wealth and influence to put together a team of eight lawyers to defend his company's rights to the Teapot Dome lease. When the trial began a year later, in March 1925, Roberts and Pomerene recognized that they were fighting an uphill battle. The biggest problem they faced was the difficulty in forcing important witnesses to testify. Sinclair was a very powerful businessman. No one wanted to testify against him. One after another, the witnesses found legal reasons for not having to testify. Without witnesses, they couldn't

convince the court to overturn the lease agreement. The result was the judge's decision in June 1925 that the lease Sinclair held was valid. It looked as if Sinclair had won.

The lawyers representing Harry Sinclair (second from left) included (from left) G.T. Stanford, J.W. Simpson, Bill Zevely, and Martin W. Littleton.

Roberts and Pomerene didn't give up, though. They appealed the decision. In September 1926, they got their victory when the appeals court overturned the previous court's decision and canceled the Teapot Dome lease and contract held by Sinclair. Sinclair had to give more than $12 million to the government.

While Sinclair was trying to maintain his oil lease, he was also facing more legal trouble. On March 31, 1924, Sinclair had been charged with contempt of Congress because of his refusal to testify before the Committee on Public Lands and Surveys. Sinclair was later found guilty and sentenced to six months in prison.

Doheny's oil lease trial began on October 21, 1924. It took the judge more than six months to hand down a decision. On May 28, 1925, the judge decided the contracts and leases to the Elk Hills reserve were cancelled. The oil reserves were returned to the U.S. government, and Doheny had to pay the government almost $35 million.

On November 22, 1926, Doheny and Fall faced a jury to answer charges that they had tried to defraud the United States. Like Sinclair, Doheny had money and influence. The jury saw hundreds of exhibits and listened to hours of witness testimony. When they returned the verdict, it was "not guilty." Despite the shocking result, Roberts and Pomerene tried once more to go after Fall. They were determined that there should be some form of justice for a government official who had taken a bribe and betrayed the American people.

Fall was charged with accepting a bribe from Doheny, and on October 7, 1928, his trial began. By this time Fall was in very poor health. He was brought into the courtroom in a wheelchair. He even collapsed at one point during the trial. More than a year later, on October 25, 1929, the jury reached its decision. One by one they were asked to give their verdict, and one by one they responded "guilty." Still, the following year, Doheny, who was charged with offering Fall the bribe, was acquitted on all counts.

Fall was sentenced to a year in prison and fined $100,000. With the jury's decision, Albert B. Fall

NOT ABOVE THE LAW

Wealthy and powerful, Harry Ford Sinclair faced a challenge to his reputation with his involvement in the Teapot Dome scandal. Like many very wealthy industrialists, he seemed to believe that he was above the law. When he was brought to trial about the Teapot Dome lease, the prosecuting attorneys informed the judge that Sinclair had hired a detective agency to follow each member of the jury. Sinclair was trying to find whatever means he could to make sure that the jury voted in his favor. Instead, the judge found Sinclair in contempt of court. Sinclair had to pay a fine and spend six months in prison.

became the first Cabinet member ever to be convicted of a felony.

The matter of Teapot Dome, Buena Vista, and Elk Hills was more than just a private moneymaking action between a representative of the U.S. government and a private business interest. The scandal raised important questions with far-reaching consequences. In his personal notes on the investigation, Pomerene described the issues the scandal raised:

Can the Naval Oil Reserves of such great value be bargained away in secret by public officials to their favorites? Can millions of barrels of royalty crude oil be delivered to these same favorites without competitive bidding, for the construction of steel tankage and for fuel oil? ... Can the public business be thus transacted and in secret? Shall men be permitted to make alleged "loans" ... to public officials with whom they are dealing for the public domain?

The Legacy of Teapot Dome

In the aftermath of the Teapot Dome scandal, North Dakota Senator Gerald Nye reflected on what he called the "the slimiest of slimy trails beaten by privilege":

> The investigation has shown, let us hope, privilege at its worst. The trail is one of dishonesty, greed, violation of law, secrecy, concealment, evasion, falsehood, and cunning. It is a trail of betrayals by trusted and presumably honorable men—betrayals of a government, of certain business interests and the people who trusted and honored them; it is a trail showing a flagrant degree of the exercise of political power and influence, and the power and influence of great wealth upon individuals and political parties; it is the trail of despoilers and schemers, far more dangerous to the well-being of our Nation and our democracy than all those who have

A political cartoon titled "Who says a watched pot never boils?" featured the U.S. Capitol as a boiling and overflowing teapot.

been deported from our shores in all time as undesirable citizens. And in the end the story is one of the crushing of brilliant careers when finally the light was played upon those who schemed those unhealthy schemes born in darkness.

The failure of Harding (left) to properly oversee the activities of his Cabinet resulted in a scandal-filled administration.

The Teapot Dome scandal has come to represent the ease with which widespread corruption and misuse of government authority can occur. The oil leases themselves were only part of the illegal activities that took place during Harding's administration. Most of his Cabinet members were involved in bribery, corruption, fraud, and other unethical activities at some time during the few years Harding was president.

The Enron Scandal

In 2001, a scandal surrounding the Enron energy company brought to light an unhealthy connection between private business and public government that led some historians to draw comparisons with the Teapot Dome scandal. In 2000, Enron donated $1.76 million to the presidential campaign of Republican candidate George W. Bush. Kenneth Lay, the chairman of the board at Enron, personally contributed more to the campaign than anyone else. After Bush's election, Enron seemed to gain a great deal of influence over U.S. government policy in areas that affected the company's profits. There has been no direct proof that Enron executives bribed government officials in order to further Enron's specific goals. However, there have been plenty of accusations, and many Americans continue to call for the appointment of a special prosecutor to investigate the matter. In the meantime, a number of high-ranking managers at Enron have been convicted of cheating their investors and employees and are serving jail time.

To this day, historians do not agree on whether Harding knew what was happening. Most historians do agree, however, that at the very least, Harding did not pay close enough attention to what his advisers were doing. Harding learned a hard lesson in realizing that government offices were not gifts to be given to friends. Because he awarded political power to those who were not qualified, he allowed them to shame the office of the president as well as betray the public trust in government officials.

However, using special prosecutors in the way they were used in the Teapot Dome scandal investigation established a precedent. To this day, investigations into possible wrongdoing by U.S. government officials are handled by special prosecutors.

The lesson of Teapot Dome is that government should not be influenced by large amounts of money offered by big business interests. Good government means government free from corruption. In the 1920s, this meant that Fall should not have taken money from the oil companies in exchange for giving them access to something that belonged to the government and the American people.

In 1999, senators Bill Bradley (left) and John McCain signed an agreement in which they promised not to receive any unregulated donations known as soft money through their political parties.

MESSAGE TO THE AMERICAN PEOPLE

We pledge that as nominees for the Office of President of the United States we will not allow our political parties to spend soft money for our presidential campaigns, and we commit to working together toward genuine campaign finance reform.

Bill Bradley

John McCain

84

The Teapot Dome scandal was the first symbol of government corruption in 20th-century America. Largely as a result of Teapot Dome, President Warren G. Harding's administration has been remembered by history as one of the most corrupt to occupy the White House. But historian Francis Busch has pointed out another important lesson of Teapot Dome that is especially important to all of us. Referring to the Teapot Dome lawsuits, he said:

> *These cases demonstrate democracy's boast that no man, rich or poor, of high or low estate, is above the law.* ◣

Timeline

1899

Warren G. Harding is elected to the Ohio state Senate; his campaign manager is Harry M. Daugherty.

1903

Harding is elected lieutenant governor of Ohio.

1904

Edwin C. Denby is elected to the U.S. House of Representatives from Michigan's 1st District.

1912

Albert B. Fall is elected to the U.S. Senate; President William Howard Taft creates the Naval Oil Reserves from 70,000 acres (28,000 hectares) of federally owned oil land in California and Wyoming.

1914

Harding is elected a U.S. senator from Ohio; World War I begins in Europe.

1915

Harding and Fall meet as fellow senators; President Woodrow Wilson sets aside both Wyoming and California oil reserves for the U.S. Navy.

1917

The United States enters World War I.

March 4, 1921

Harding is inaugurated as the 23rd president of the United States; he begins building his Cabinet when he appoints Denby as secretary of the Navy, Fall as secretary of the interior, and Daugherty as U.S. attorney general.

May 31, 1921

Harding signs Executive Order Number 3474, transferring authority for oil reserve properties from the Navy Department to the Department of the Interior.

November 30, 1921

Oil company executive Edward L. Doheny lends $100,000 to his friend Fall.

April 7, 1922

Fall secretly leases the Teapot Dome oil field to Harry F. Sinclair.

April 14, 1922

The Wall Street Journal breaks the story that Fall secretly leased oil reserves to private business interests.

April 15, 1922

The Senate passes Resolution 277, which asks Denby and Fall whether leases had been given on the government-owned oil reserves.

April 25, 1922

Fall gives Doheny the rights to drill for oil in the California oil reserves through a secret lease agreement.

April 29, 1922

The Senate passes Resolution 282, which provides for a special investigation into the lease agreements; Senator Thomas J. Walsh

of Montana is appointed head of the Senate subcommittee charged with investigating the possible illegal leasing of the oil reserves.

May 13, 1922

Senator Robert La Follette reads to the Senate a letter of protest from the oil industry regarding the possibility that oil reserves been illegally leased.

March 4, 1923

Fall resigns as secretary of the interior.

August 2, 1923

When President Harding dies in San Francisco, California, Vice President Calvin Coolidge is sworn in as president.

October 15, 1923

The Senate Committee on Public Lands and Surveys begins hearings on the California and Teapot Dome oil leases.

October 23, 1923

Fall is called to testify before the Senate subcommittee.

January 24, 1924

Doheny admits giving Fall a $100,000 loan.

January 27, 1924

President Coolidge announces that he will appoint two special prosecutors to investigate the accusations that Fall accepted bribes to lease oil reserves to private business interests.

February 16, 1924

The U.S. Senate confirms the appointment of Owen Roberts and Atlee Pomerene as special prosecutors charged with investigating whether Fall accepted bribes to grant oil reserve leases to Doheny and Sinclair.

Timeline

February 18, 1924

Denby resigns as secretary of the Navy.

March 13, 1924

Special prosecutors file a lawsuit against Sinclair's Mammoth Oil Company.

March 28, 1924

Daugherty resigns as U.S. attorney general.

March 31, 1924

Sinclar is charged with contempt of Congress for his refusal to testify before the committee; he is later found guilty and sentenced to six months in prison.

June 30, 1924

Special prosecutors Roberts and Pomerene gain indictments against Fall, Doheny, and Sinclair.

October 21, 1924

Doheny's oil lease trial begins.

May 28, 1925

The judge in Doheny's trial cancels the contracts and leases to the Elk Hills reserve, returning the reserve to the U.S. government.

November 22, 1926

Doheny and Fall answer charges of trying to defraud the U.S. government; they are later found not guilty.

October 10, 1927

The U.S. Supreme Court rules in the Sinclair oil lease trial, restoring the Teapot Dome reserve to the federal government.

October 25, 1929

Fall is convicted of bribery and receives a one-year prison sentence and a $100,000 fine.

March 22, 1930

Doheny is acquitted of bribery.

On the Web

For more information on this topic, use FactHound.

1 Go to *www.facthound.com*

2 Type in this book ID: 0756533368

3 Click on the *Fetch It!* button. FactHound will find the best Web sites for you.

Historic Sites

Harding Home and Tomb State Memorial
380 Mount Vernon Ave.
Marion, Ohio 43302
740/387-9630

This National Historic Landmark features a museum in the Press House, a building at the rear of the home that served as Harding's campaign headquarters.

The U.S. Capitol
Washington, D.C. 20510
202/225-6827

Tours of the Capitol building are available, and visitors can watch the U.S. Senate in action in the Capitol Galleries.

Look for More Books in This Series

The Berlin Wall:
Barrier to Freedom

Black Tuesday:
Prelude to the Great Depression

A Day Without Immigrants:
Rallying Behind America's Newcomers

Freedom Rides:
Campaign for Equality

The March on Washington:
Uniting Against Racism

The National Grape Boycott:
A Victory for Farmworkers

Third Parties:
Influential Political Alternatives

A complete list of **Snapshots in History** titles is available on our Web site: *www.compasspointbooks.com*

Glossary

blackmailer
person who forces someone to do
something by threatening to tell things
that would harm his or her reputation

bribe
give someone money or gifts to persuade
him or her to do a particular thing,
especially something illegal or dishonest

corruption
dishonesty or misuse of power for
personal gain

graft
illegal practice such as bribery used to
secure gains in politics or business

inauguration
formal ceremony used to swear a person
into political office

lease
rent property or resources to someone for
a period of time

lobbyist
person who is paid to influence political
policy on a particular issue

materialist
someone who is concerned about
wealth and material goods more than
anything else

oil baron
person who has made a large fortune
in the oil industry and who influences
government policy

patronage
special jobs or favors a politician gives to
loyal supporters

petroleum
raw oil that is found in rocks

political boss
leader of a political party who controls
votes, dictates appointments, and
influences government decisions

political scandal
event within the government that causes
the public to become angry

Prohibition
the forbidding by law of the manufacture,
sale, or transport of alcoholic beverages in
the United States from 1920 to 1933

prosecutor
lawyer who represents the government in
a criminal trial

reserves
materials held back, or saved, for later use

subcommittee
group that is set up to deal with a
particular issue

unsavory
unpleasant

Source Notes

Chapter 2

Page 25, line 8: Robert K. Murray. "Warren G. Harding." Profiles of U.S. Presidents. 25 April 2007. www.presidentprofiles.com/Grant-Eisenhower/Harding-Warren-G.html

Chapter 3

Page 33, line 21: Bruce Bliven. "Tempest Over Teapot." AmericanHeritage.com August 1965. 25 April 2007. www.americanheritage.com/articles/magazine/ah/1965/5/1965_5_20.shtml

Chapter 4

Page 36, line 3: Leslie E. Bennett. "One Lesson From History: Appointment of Special Counsel and the Investigation of the Teapot Dome Scandal." The Brookings Institution. 1999. 25 April 2007. www.brook.edu/gs/ic/teapotdome/teapotdome.htm

Page 42, line 27: Sanford J. Mock. "Tempest Beyond the Teapot." Financial History.org 1996. 25 Apr. 2007. www.financialhistory.org/fh/1996/54-1.html

Chapter 5

Page 52, line 7: "One Lesson From History: Appointment of Special Counsel and the Investigation of the Teapot Dome Scandal."

Page 53, line 1: Ibid.

Page 54, line 16: "Tempest Beyond the Teapot."

Page 55, sidebar: Francis Russell. "The Four Mysteries of Warren Harding." AmericanHeritage.com April 1963. 15 May 2007. www.americanheritage.com/articles/magazine/ah/1963/3/1963_3_4.shtml

Chapter 6

Page 64, line 5: Ibid.

SOURCE NOTES

Chapter 7

Page 67, line 2: "One Lesson From History: Appointment of Special Counsel and the Investigation of the Teapot Dome Scandal."

Page 68, line 19: Ibid.

Page 70, line 9: Ibid.

Page 71, line 1: Ibid.

Page 74, line 4: Ibid.

Page 74, line 22: Ibid.

Page 74, line 4: Ibid.

Page 74, line 22: Ibid.

Page 79, line 11: Ibid.

Chapter 8

Page 80, line 3: Ibid.

Page 80, line 5: Ibid.

Page 85, line 10: Ibid.

SELECT BIBLIOGRAPHY

Anthony, Carl Sferrazza. *Florence Harding.* New York: William Morrow and Company, 1998.

Davis, Margaret L. *Dark Side of Fortune: Triumph and Scandal in the Life of Oil Tycoon Edward L. Doheny.* Berkeley: University of California Press, 1998.

Dean, John W. *Warren G. Harding.* New York: Henry Holt and Company, 2004.

Noggle, Burl. *Teapot Dome: Oil and Politics in the 1920s.* Westport, Conn.: Greenwood Press, 1980.

Stratton, David H. *Tempest Over Teapot Dome: The Story of Albert B. Fall.* Norman: University of Oklahoma Press, 1998.

Weisner, Herman B. *The Politics of Justice: A.B. Fall and the Teapot Dome Scandal: A New Perspective.* Albuquerque, N.M.: Creative Designs, 1988.

Wukovits, John F., ed. *The 1920s.* San Diego: Greenhaven Press Inc., 2000.

FURTHER READING

Landau, Elaine. *Warren G. Harding.* Minneapolis: Lerner Publications, 2005.

Roberts, Russell. *Presidents and Scandals.* San Diego: Lucent Books, 2001.

Somervill, Barbara A. *Warren G. Harding.* Minneapolis: Compass Point Books, 2004.

Thorndike, Jonathan L. *The Teapot Dome Scandal Trial: A Headline Court Case.* Berkeley Heights, N.J.: Enslow Publishers, 2001.

Index

ABOUT THE AUTHOR

Barbara J. Davis has been writing children's nonfiction for more than 20 years. Her specialties are science, history, and nature topics. She lives in Hinckley, Minnesota. Her hobbies are reading, working with rescue dogs, and riding her horse, Wing.

IMAGE CREDITS